Score

FLOWER DUET
from Lakmé

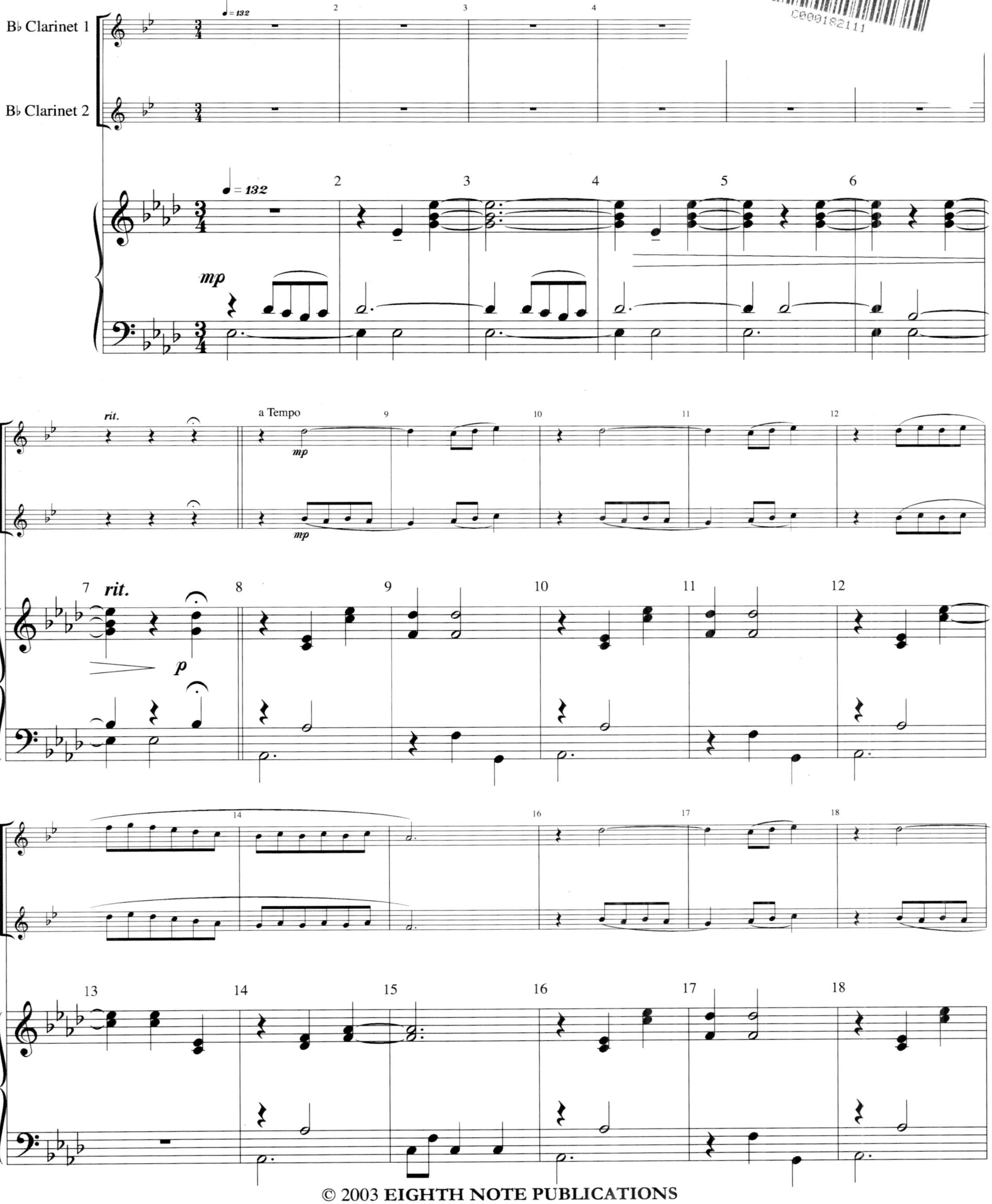

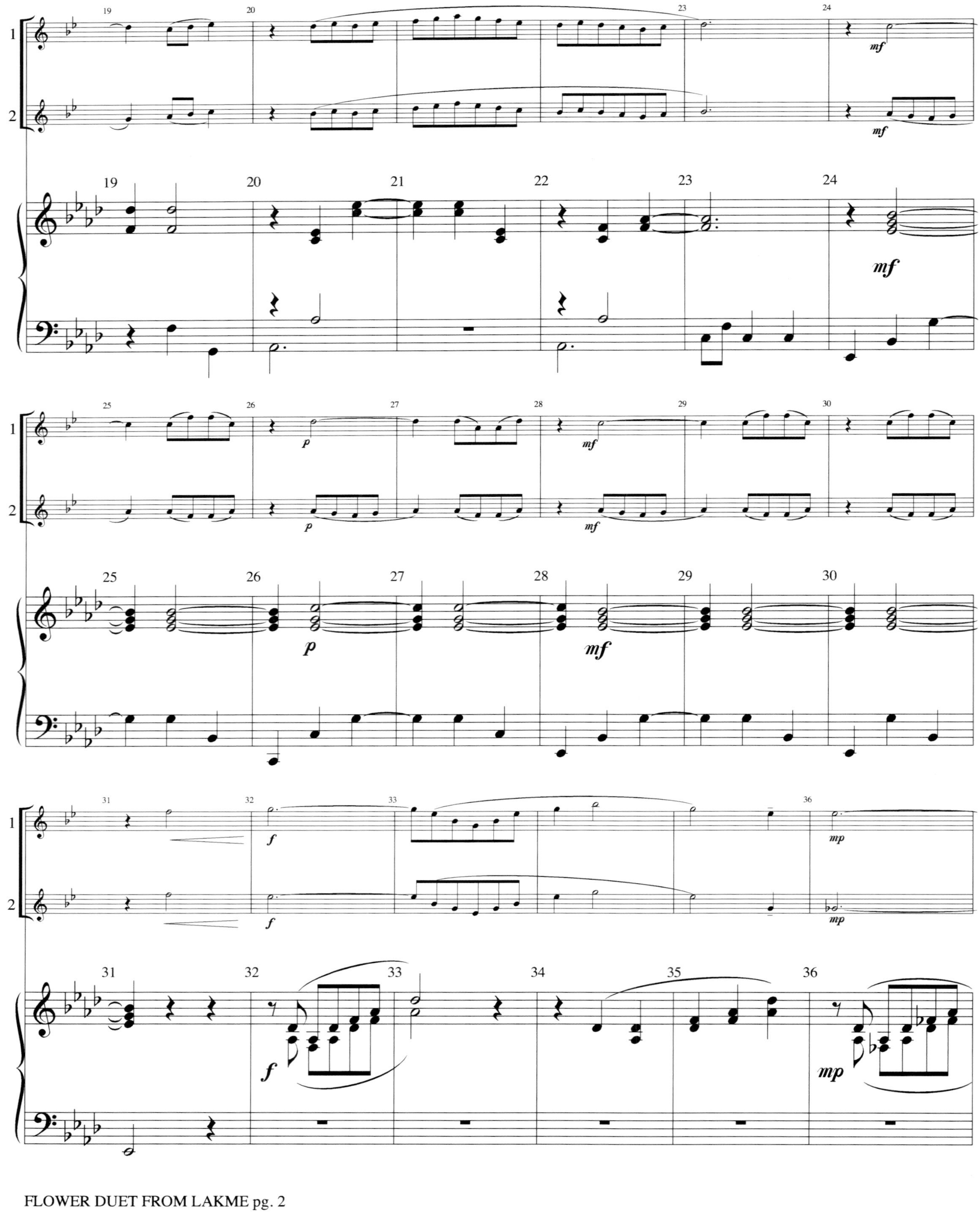

DUET
from Lakmé

L. Delibes
(1836-1891)
Arranged by D. Marlatt

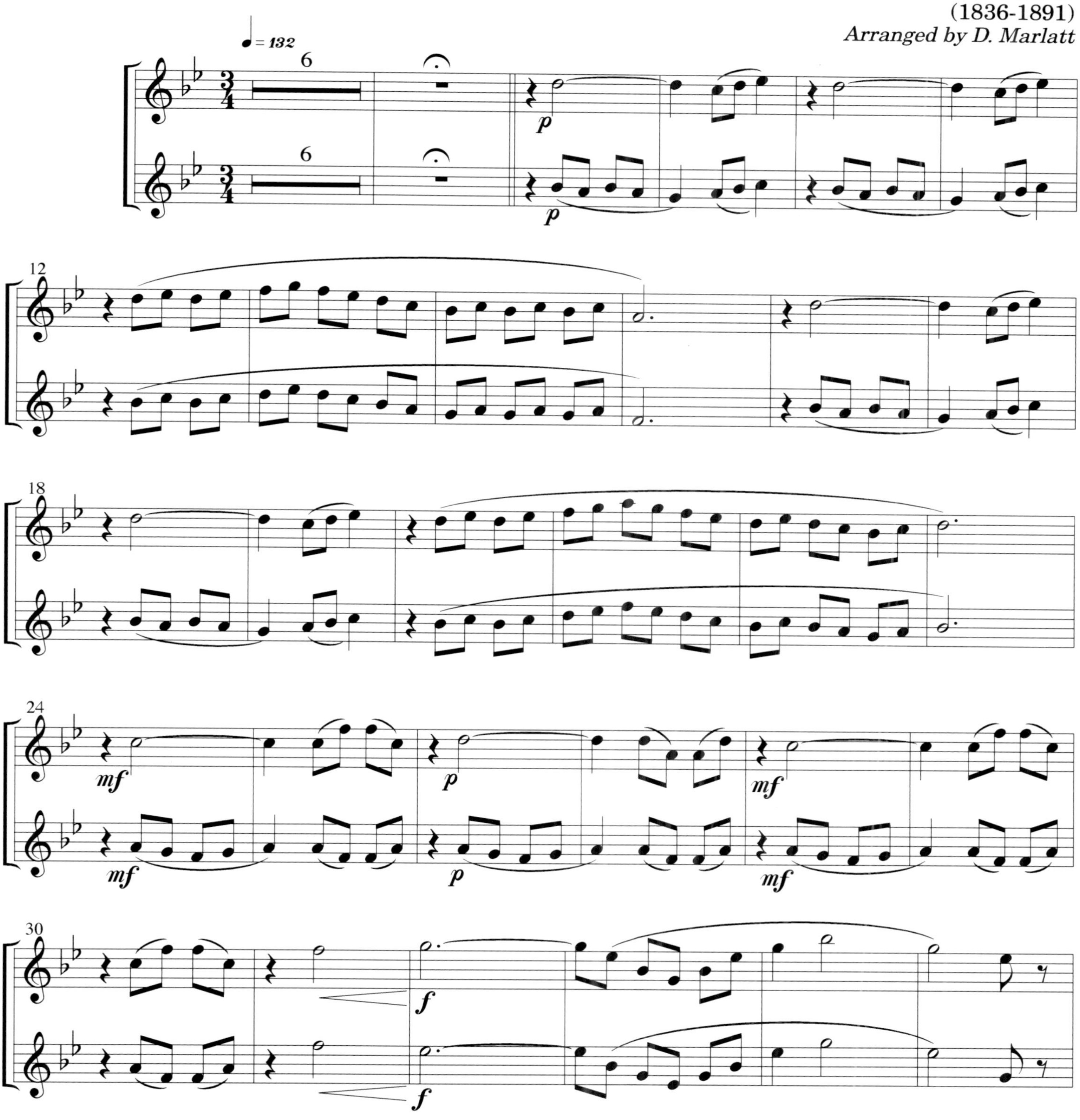

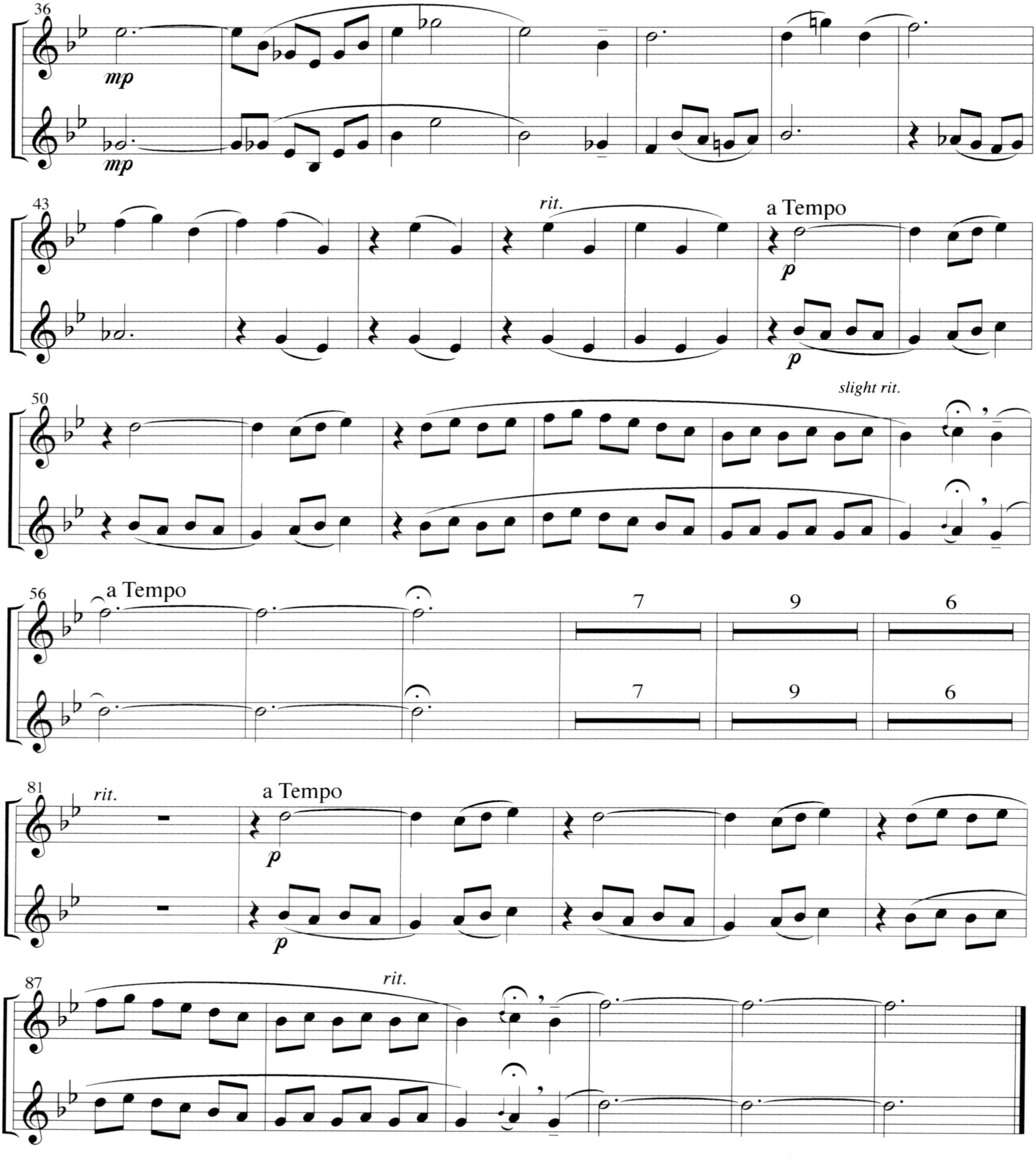
36
mp
mp
43
rit.
a Tempo
p
p
50
slight rit.
56
a Tempo
7
9
6
7
9
6
81
rit.
a Tempo
p
p
87
rit.

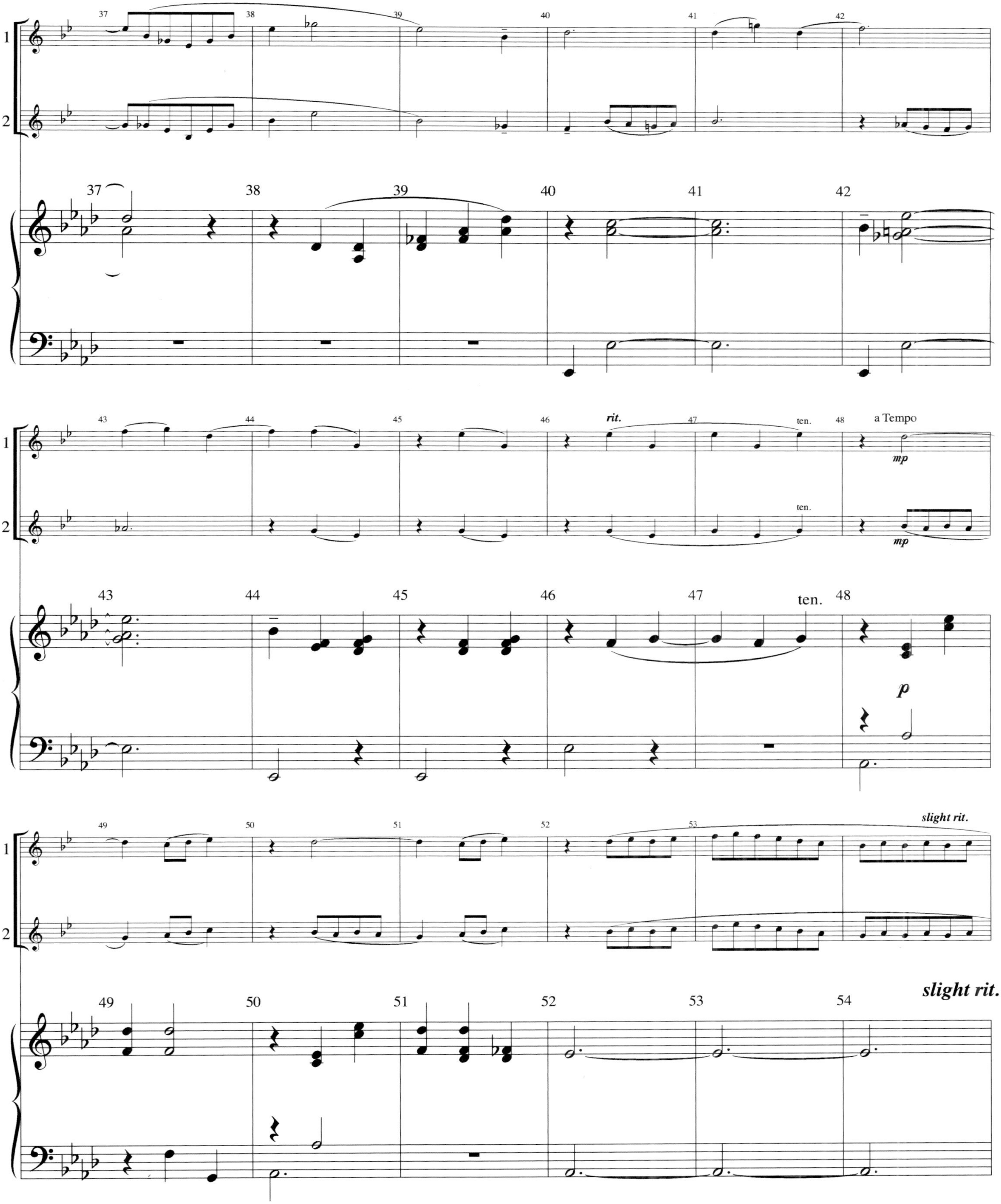
rit.
ten.
a Tempo
mp
p
slight rit.

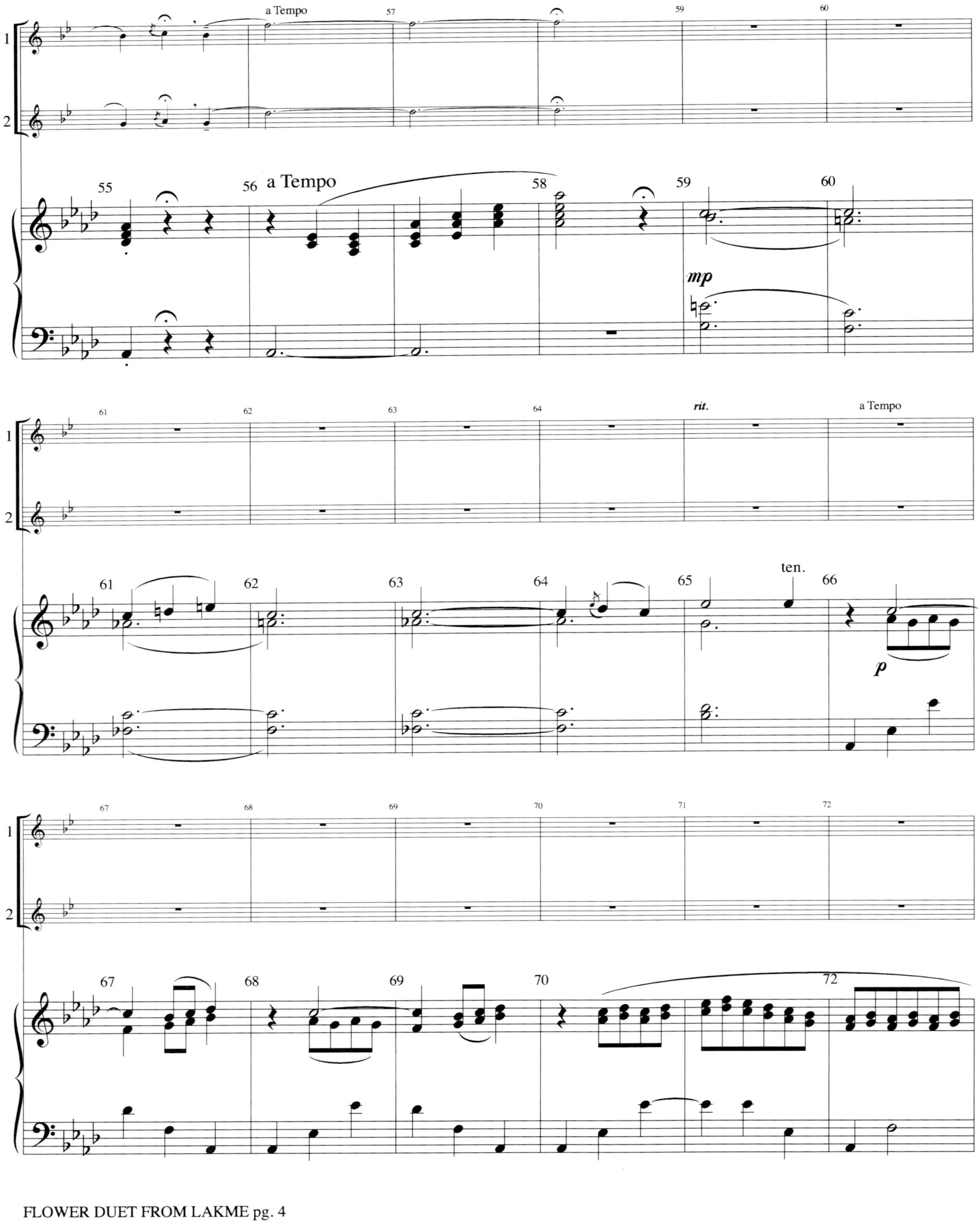

a Tempo
rit.
a Tempo
ten.
mp
p